THIS BOOK IS DEDICATED TO

My own little "Rhode Island Red," Gwen
My amazing husband &
My wonderful family and friends

I is for

To: Baby Mangiocca
Love: Aunty Cara & Uncle Mike

RI LOVES

WRITTEN AND ILLUSTRATED BY JILL AUSTIN

a
is for ANCHOR

RI LOVES to go fishing.
And an anchor will help us to stay.
Right in the spot where the fish are,
so we don't go drifting away.

b is for BASEBALL

RI LOVES to root for the PawSox. At McCoy is where they'll be. A seat on the line, a homerun in the ninth, it's a summertime sight to see.

C is for
CAROUSEL

RI LOVES its carousels. The cool breeze on our face. We ride these painted horses in a never ending race.

d is for DONUT

RI LOVES good donuts.
Whether glazed or with sprinkles on top.
On the way to the beach, to work or the store.
There are so many great reasons to stop.

e is for EAT (& DRINK)

RI LOVES to eat seafood, pizza, clam chowda' and more.
Have some coffee milk to wash it all down.
In the city or down by the shore.

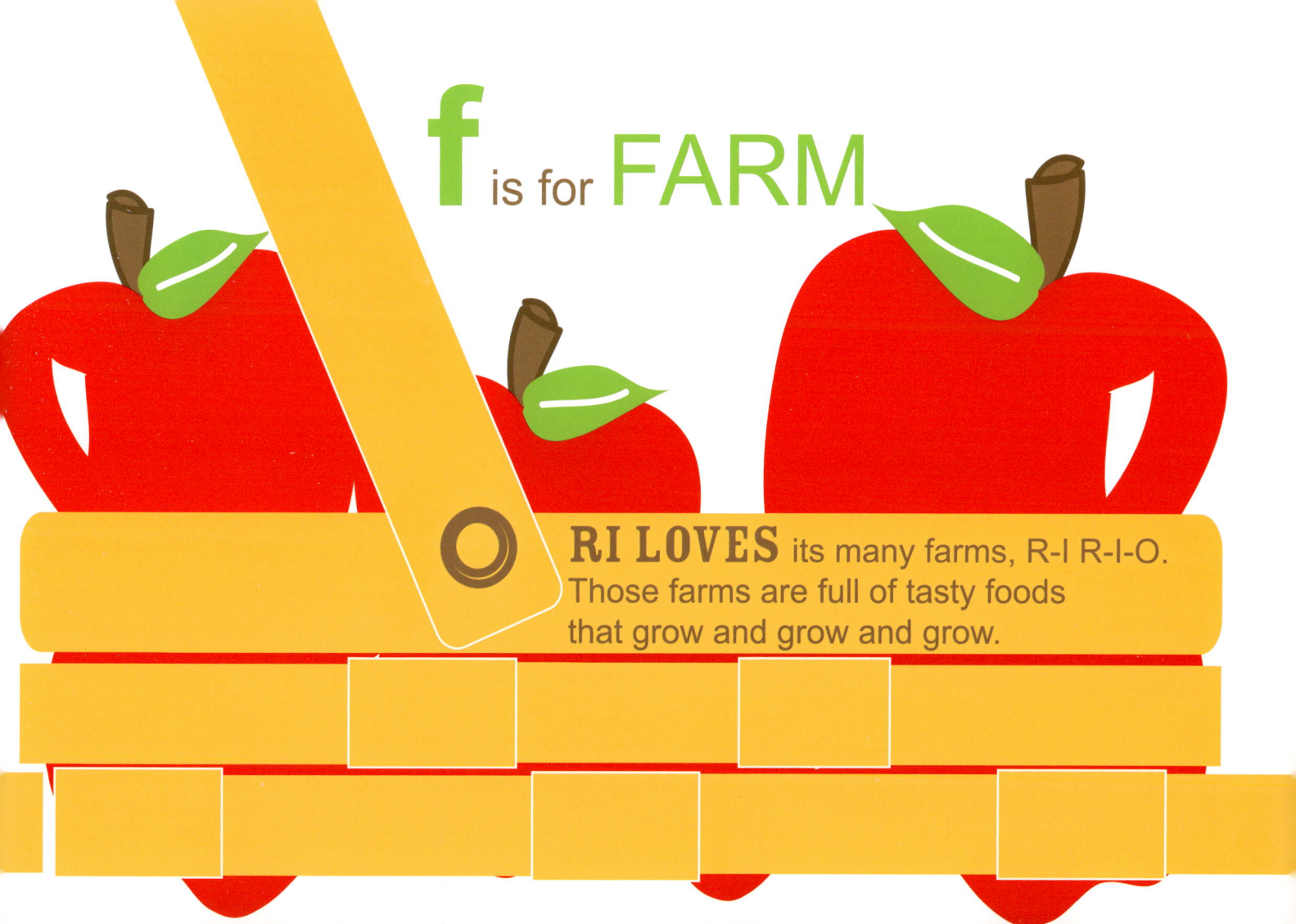

g is for **GATE**

RI LOVES these iron gates.
In Newport they're easy to find.
They line the streets of Bellevue Ave
with mansions hidden behind.

h is for HOPE

RI LOVES its motto.
It's spoken from the heart.
This little word is simply
where all dreams get their start.

i is for
INDEPENDENT MAN

RI LOVES this special guy.
He's open minded, brave and strong.
Like an ever present superhero,
here to right what's wrong.

j is for JAZZ (AND FOLK FEST)

RI LOVES great music.
By the sea it fills the air.
It's truly something you've got to see,
but more importantly hear.

k is for KNOWLEDGE

RI LOVES to learn and grow and do its academic best.
When it comes to achieving great things, we always pass the test.

L is for LEMONADE

RI LOVES this icy treat. It's refreshingly different and great in the heat. Whether you sip from the cup or scoop with a spoon, once you run out you'll be coming back soon.

RI LOVES
its Big Blue friend.
He's surely not a pest.
He watches over 95
from his cozy rooftop nest.

n is for NIBBLES woodaway

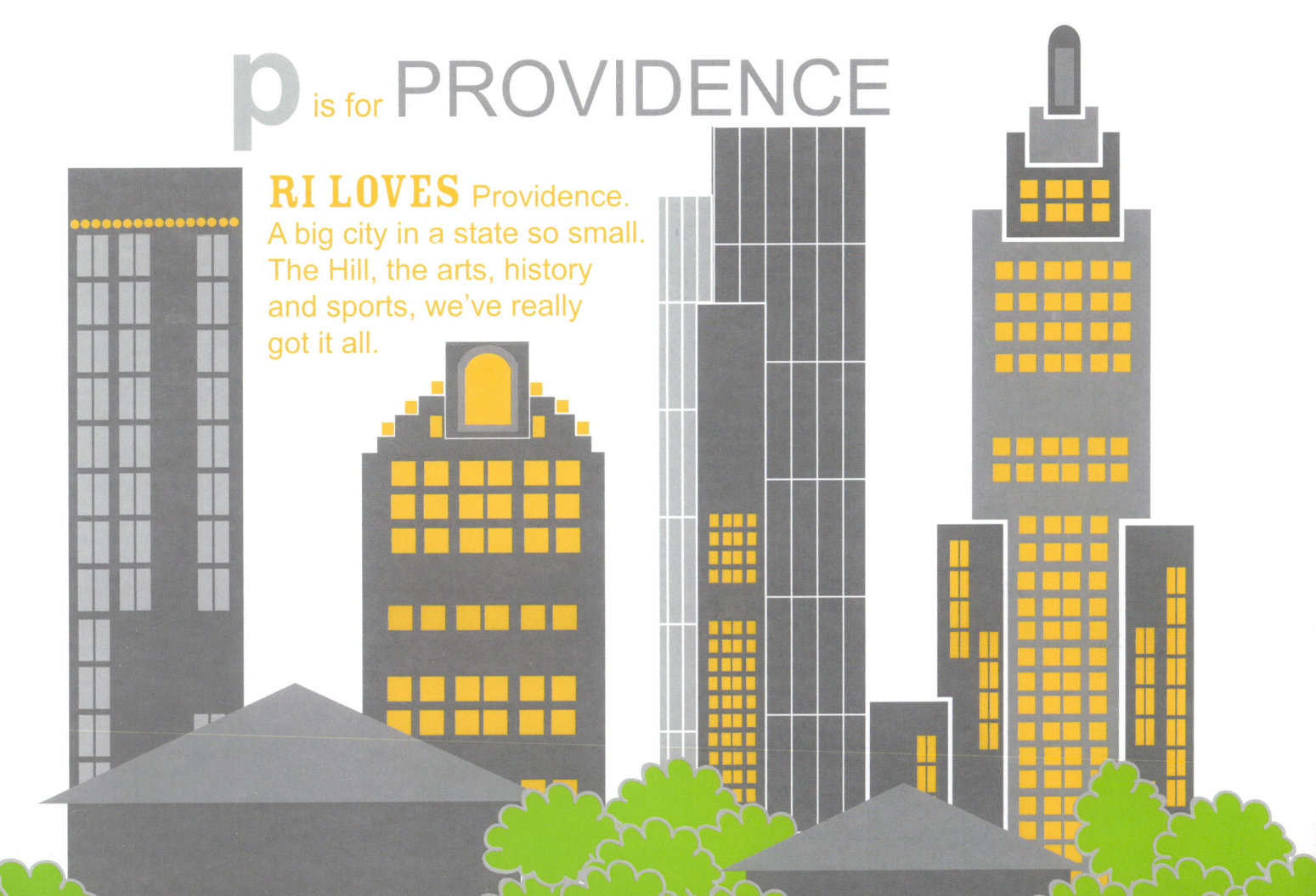

q is for QUAHOG

RI LOVES its state shellfish.
In chowder, cakes and in sauce.
Some call them a clam, but what's in a name?
We all know that they're quahogs, of course.

r is for

ROCKY POINT

RI LOVES tradition, with family & with friends. The Corkscrew and The Flume meant it was summertime again.

W is for WEATHER

RI LOVES to talk weather.
Ask anyone you see.
The summers are too hot, the winters are too cold.
But there's no place that we'd rather be.

X is for X GAMES

RI LOVES to be extreme. So it wasn't hard to see. That Providence would be the first place these games were set to be.

YOUR TOUR through Rhody's over. But there's so much more to be found. In a state so small, with a heart so big, we're sure to see you around.

SPECIAL THANKS TO THE FOLLOWING

Autocrat Coffee Syrup
Big Blue Bug Solutions
Brown University
Bryant University
Community College of Rhode Island
Del's Lemonade
ESPN's X Games
Johnson and Wales University
Newport Festivals Foundation
Pawtucket Red Sox
Providence College
Rhode Island College
Rhode Island School of Design
Roger Williams Park Zoo
Roger Williams University
Salve Regina University
University of Rhode Island
Yacht Club Soda

t is for THANK YOU